FATHERLESS DAUGHTER

A Journey to HealingTheKasha1985

Dr. Rokasha Edmondson

Copyright © 2024 by Rokasha Edmondson.

All rights reserved. No part of this book may be used or reproduced in any form whatsoever without written permission except in the case of brief quotations in critical articles or reviews.

Printed in the United States of America.

For more information, or to book an event, contact : missrofcc@gmail.com

Book design by Rokasha Edmondson
Cover design by Elliot Lea

ISBN - Paperback: 9798879138832
First Edition: February 2024

To my grandmother, Gloria Edmondson.
Who wiped my tears and rubbed my back when daddy did not come.

To my dad.
Thank you for not giving up and being an amazing grandfather.

To my sister, Ebony.
Thank you for sharing your truth with me so that I could walk in mine.

CONTENTS

PREFACE. 6
FIRST CHAPTER 8
SECOND CHAPTER 10
THIRD CHAPTER 13
FOURTH CHAPTER 6
FIFTH CHAPTER 18
SIXTH CHAPTER 21
ABOUT THE AUTHOR 26
ACKNOWLEDGEMENTS 27

PREFACE

This book is for all daughters. For daughters without fathers. For daughters with fathers in their homes. For daughters who felt abandoned. For daughters who felt overlooked. For daughters who felt empty. For daughters who lacked guidance. For daughters who simply desired a father's love. It is for girls who have grown into women but felt something was missing on the journey. The aim is not to diminish men who have aided in creating a daughter but to help those who felt fatherless at any moment. It includes a narrative of accounts of my life as I reflect on my pilgrimage from childhood to adulthood and my relationship with my father. This memoir will help all daughters work to reflect, heal, and forgive.

I am learning to tap into my divine feminine, Goddess energy. I grew up raised by women. All I saw were women having to be vigorous, firm, and stark. Women had to play both roles; in my experience, women appeared to be rugged and masculine. Love was present, but that softness and tenderness were lacking. So, when I speak about tapping into my divine feminine energy, it is not a reflection of the out. See, the women who raised me were beautiful and soft in appearance but on the inside hard. I now recognize that it shaped my perception of what a woman was and my ideas about men.

How can you trust a man to lead if you have never experienced a man in this way? How can you trust a man to provide when you have experienced the women in your life working until they are fragmented and mangled to ensure you are taken care of and then keep pushing? How can you trust a man to protect you when no man was there to protect you from another's touch? How can you trust love when your representation is problematic, and there are no men in your life to show you what love should look like? No woman wants to be callous or perceived to be complicated. Being independent is good, but it would be nice to avoid carrying the load. At least not me. It is through her own experiences that her vision has been obscured and overshadowed. Now, she chooses to release and surrender in preparation for her new journey of self, love, and femineity. A journey of healing and rewriting the tale of what it looks like to be a fatherless daughter.

ROKASHA EDMONDSON

CHAPTER 1

WINDOW WATCHING

"IN THE BEGINNING, GOD CREATED THE HEAVEN AND THE EARTH" (KING JAMES BIBLE, 1769/2023, GENESIS 1:1).

The beginning. Returning to the start would mean facing my earliest memory of my father. I was a little girl living in the small town of South Boston, Virginia, in a white house with my grandmother and mother on North Main Street. I couldn't have been more than five years old. The only reminiscence of my father in the home was some speakers he had from his career as a disc jockey. I knew because I asked what they were and wanted to touch them. My grandmother would say, "Don't touch them. Them Yō daddy's." Which was confusing because I was the one who had to dust them on Saturday mornings.

One day I got a call. It was a call from my father. I sat on the living room floor, talking to my father on our white rotary phone. I was excited hearing him talk about wanting to do a music video and having my cousins, my sister, and myself as a part of the video. Finally, the day had arrived. The day daddy was coming. I woke up early that morning, anticipating his arrival with excitement. With every sound and bump I heard, I peeked at the window. I'm just sure it was Daddy at the door. Breakfast passed, lunch passed, and dinner passed, and I still anxiously ran to the window beside the door. As night fell, I sat by the door and waited. My bedtime came, and my grandmother said, "He's not coming; no need to keep looking. Come and get in the bed." She must have been mistaken. I know what Daddy told me. Daddy said he was coming. I must have stayed there all-night waiting, but Daddy never came.

That was the beginning. My beginning. Window-watching for my father was my first experience with heartbreak. Window-watching for

FATHERLESS DAUGHTERS

Daddy was the first time a man broke my heart. Window-watching for Dad was my first lesson on men and trust. They will not show up. They lie. They will break your heart—my first realization of being a fatherless daughter.

CHAPTER 2

WHERE ARE YOU?

"THOUGH HE SLAY ME, YET WILL I TRUST IN HIM: BUT I WILL MAINTAIN MINE OWN WAYS BEFORE HIM" (KING JAMES BIBLE, 1769/2023, JOB 13:15).

A synonym for the word slay is destroyed or done away with. The start of my fourth-grade school year was precisely when I felt my life had been destroyed. The way I knew life to be forever changed. I lived in an apartment complex with my grandmother and my mother in Danville, Virginia. My grandmother and I shared a room just like we always did. I didn't mind it. We talked about everything until one day. Well, one day, I was walking up the stairs and went to say something to my mother, but when I peeked into her bedroom, I saw her weeping. I heard her sobbing and saw the tears flow down her face. I quietly closed the door and went to my grandmother. I asked her why my mommy was crying, and she said, "If she wanted you to know, she would tell you." Her crying made me cry. I quietly turned to the wall in the bed that my grandmother and I shared and let the water roll down my face until I fell asleep.

Quickly after seeing my mother cry, things began to shift. My mother began packing our house, but I noticed she mostly gave everything away. I remember having this huge closet full of toys. Afterward, I was left with my bright-colored duffle bag of dolls and accessories. To this day, I still collect those dolls. We had lost everything. I was lost and confused. My child's brain didn't understand what was happening. After that day, my grandmother and I never shared the same bed again. My mother and I went to stay with one of her friends, and my grandmother found herself in affordable housing for the elderly. After that day, I never saw my mother weep again. She dragged me to church, prayer service, Sunday school, and Bible study weekly. Those around us mocked and laughed, but she never gave up. She kept the faith.

Growing up during my time, you didn't get too much in adult business or ask too many questions. See, I had questions. Though I was a child, I didn't understand why my mother was alone. She worked hard to care for me then, but her best wasn't enough. Why did she have to carry this burden alone? Where was my father? At this moment, life taught me that anyone could abandon you, even your father. So here I learned it's easy for a man to leave you behind or relinquish any responsibility. It was another reminder that I was a fatherless daughter.

CHAPTER 3

CYCLES

"FOR PHARAOH WILL SAY OF THE CHILDREN OF ISRAEL, THEY ARE ENTANGLED IN THE LAND, THE WILDERNESS HATH SHUT THEM IN" (KING JAMES BIBLE, 1769/2023, EXODUS 14:3).

Cycles. As a child, when going to the laundry mat with my Aunt Mae, I remember looking at the clothes in the dryer. They were being tossed around and around in what appeared to be an endless repeating pattern. Moving in a cycle. That's what life felt like. Because here I was, headed into the 6th grade, and we had moved several times, and I had lived with several people, but we still didn't have a place to call our own. I would go to school and wonder what it was like for the other children at home. Did they have their own room? Did they share a bed with their mom like I did? Did they come home from school and wash their clothes in the tub on

Monday so they would have something clean to wear on Wednesday? Indeed, their lives were very different. I wanted so badly to be like the others. You know. To simply fit in.

At the time, my mother was facing a hard time financially, and the last place we were staying was no longer an option. I'm sure this was our third location since Grandma no longer lived with us. The sweetest lady from our church allowed us to stay with her, her son, and her brother. Her entire family embraced us and treated us like family. I loved it when she would cook lasagna and cornbread. It was the best. Her cornbread tasted like pound cake.

Christmas had come, and my mom allowed me to visit with my dad for winter break. My dad had come and picked me up, and I was excited. I was mostly excited about seeing my twin sister. Well, we weren't twins. We were eight months apart, but everyone thought we were twins. We drove off, and my excitement quickly dwindled as my dad spoke, "Your momma told me she would chase me around until I lived in a cardboard box. Look like where y'all living is a cardboard box." Really! Did he say that? Those words still crush me to this day. This was my home. The place that I lived. A place that someone else provided when you didn't. That day, at twelve-years- old, I no longer viewed Dad from a little girl's eyes. That day, Dad became selfish, egocentric, and narrow-minded. Did you want to win a battle with my mom so much that you would do it at the expense of hurting me? Yes, because that day, Daddy pulled me again and taught me another lesson. Daddy taught me that it will always be the closest to you and the ones you love most that will bring the most pain. Daddy taught me that being collateral damage in other people's drama is a part of life. Daddy taught me that no one's feelings were off limit, not even mine. That day, Daddy's presence gave me the painful lesson of being a fatherless daughter.

CHAPTER 4

HE TOUCHED ME

"YEA, LET NONE THAT WAIT ON THEE BE ASHAMED: LET THEM BE ASHAMED WHICH TRANSGRESS WITHOUT CAUSE" (KING JAMES BIBLE, 1769/2023, PSALM 25:3).

He touched me. Oh, he touched me. I can still hear the choir singing it because this song, well, it haunts me. But to this day, the only image I see when going back to that moment is my grandma in the choir, standing in her black and white robe. Maybe it's because my grandmother was my safety net and place of peace. I'm not sure, but on that day, the touch I felt wasn't God's hand but a touch that left me ashamed, fearful, and hopeless.

A child. Only a child. As an adult, I reflect; that's all I can think of. I was just a child. Frightened, I closed my eyes and drifted into the darkness as if I could no longer be seen. It was clear that closing my eyes wasn't a magical disappearing act, and there was no escape. So, with my eyes still closed and holding on to the darkness, I kicked. I kicked fiercely, fighting as my pants dropped to my knees. Then to my ankles. I screamed, and I yelled, but no one came for me. He must have gotten tired of me clawing and kicking like a wild animal or screeching like a barred owl at night, or maybe Grandma's prayers saved me that day. I'll never know.

That day, I felt unprotected. Where was my father? Why wasn't he there to protect me from another's touch? How could he let this happen to his baby girl? That day, I learned that the world was cruel and that I was alone. I was reminded that I couldn't call Daddy for protection because Daddy wasn't there. I learned that neither my body nor I was special; it was just there for some guy to share. I perceived that Daddy was living his life and didn't care. I was reminded that I didn't have a dad present to protect me. I was reminded that I was a fatherless daughter.

CHAPTER 5

DADDY'S GIRL OR A FATHER'S WORSE NIGHTMARE

"NOTWITHSTANDING, I HAVE A FEW THINGS AGAINST THEE BECAUSE THOU SUFFEREST THAT WOMAN JEZEBEL, WHICH CALLETH HERSELF A PROPHETESS, TO TEACH AND TO SEDUCE MY SERVANTS TO COMMIT FORNICATION, AND TO EAT THINGS SACRIFICED UNTO IDOLS. AND I GAVE HER SPACE TO REPENT OF HER FORNICATION, AND SHE REPENTED NOT. BEHOLD, I WILL

FATHERLESS DAUGHTERS

CAST HER INTO A BED, AND THEM THAT COMMIT ADULTERY WITH HER INTO GREAT TRIBULATION, EXCEPT THEY REPENT OF THEIR DEEDS."
(KING JAMES BIBLE, 1769/2023, REVELATION 2:20-22).

Young adulthood. That time in life where legally you're grown, and expectations are placed on you that you're not quite prepared for as you don't know entirely what you're doing or who you are. Am I a child? Am I an adult? You can be at any moment, depending on the day. In June, I walked across the stage as a high school graduate, and by July, I found a 17-year-old me on a college campus with nothing—no money, no guidance, no resources, and unprepared. Young adult me. Unhealed me. I was pushed into the world with the lessons that Daddy had taught me. This was the start of my dissolution. The curtains were off, and I stepped out confidently onto the stage, showing the world who I was. I sang, was on the cheer squad, was on the student activity council, started a dance squad, and even put on a talent showcase that supported community efforts. But underneath all that was still the girl who was lost, hurting, and looking to fill an emptiness that had been present since she was five.

By the start of my sophomore year of college, I found myself pregnant and alone. I lay miserably on my bed in the campus apartments, and the phone rang. It was my dad. He asked me if there was something that I needed to tell him, and I responded no. My cousin had heard the news from someone and decided it was her duty to tell my dad that I was pregnant. I was clueless, lost, and unprepared, and I found myself living in the projects with a sick baby, literally playing life by ear.

I had conformed to my new life. I was doing what a mother had to do. I heard my name and walked onto the stage. And there, sitting in the back, was my son's father. So, there I was disgraced. Not ashamed that I was going to shake a little ass for some change, but ashamed that my sons' father was in the audience spending money on booze and dances while I did so.

My unemotional response to my son's father's absence and antics confused people. Somehow or another, I was at peace with it. Well, my soul expected it. Did my father teach me any difference? You see, that was another moment in my life where I had materialized that I was a fatherless daughter.

CHAPTER 6

FORGIVENESS

FOR IF YE FORGIVE MEN THEIR TRESPASSES, YOUR HEAVENLY FATHER WILL ALSO FORGIVE YOU: BUT IF YE FORGIVE NOT MEN THEIR TRESPASSES, NEITHER WILL YOUR FATHER FORGIVE YOUR TRESPASSES. (KING JAMES BIBLE, 1769/2023, two daughters are only a few months apart. Yep, two Baby mothers. I was a DJ and working then. Plus, after-work activities. Being a father with two daughters and not day to day in their lives keeps you wondering. How are they doing, what are they doing, do they miss me? Yet we stayed close. I was a great "weekend", Dad. Creating memories that didn't cost much money. I am blessed to have those memories to reflect on and discuss with them. But the things I missed out on. They are growing up. Happy times, sad times, friends, school activities, turning of age, and much more. It hurts to this day!!!!!

What caught my attention most in the conversation was the anxiousness combined with the pain in his voice when he mentioned his father. In the past, my dad has always talked about how amazing his father was. When I tried to scaffold to persuade him to speak more about his childhood and his father, he hesitated and quickly shifted the conversation. I felt his pain. He hurt. My dad was human, and he felt just like me. The truth is that knowing and understanding my father's story, I realized that after the first 12 years of his life, he was left a fatherless son. On November

22, 2023, in a normal conversation with my dad, I finally said, "I forgive you."

Doing the work on self is not easy. It is hard to stare at the image in the mirror and take a strong look at the person starring back. Looking at the soul of yourself. Your choices, your afflictions, and the unhealed wounds. To be honest with yourself, uncovering the hurt, the shame, while no longer hiding behind the mask of it all. It was the time to do the work and release. It took thirteen years from the start of my journey to stand in my complete nakedness and confess my truths. Some may say that is a long time. I say, it is my journey. I am thankful that I started and did not quick, but I am forever grateful that God kept my father on this side of heaven so that I could do so.

MY PURPOSE WAS CONNECTED TO MY PAIN. THE WISDOM I GAINED WAS CONNECTED TO MY WOUNDS, AND WHERE I ONCE SAW THE STRUGGLE, I NOW SEE STRENGTH. THOUGH EACH LESSON WAS PROFITABLE, I'VE LEARNED THAT CYCLES ARE REAL, AND

ROKASHA EDMONDSON

MY SOUL CANNOT AFFORD TO ALLOW ANYTHING I HAVE ALREADY HEALED INTO MY SPACE. NO MORE CYCLES. ONLY FORWARD! TRUE FORGIVENESS OCCURRED WHEN I REALIZED I WENT FROM A FATHERLESS DAUGHTER TO RAISING FATHERLESS SONS.

About the Author

Dr. Rokasha Edmondson is a mother of two boys, educator, and mentor who enjoys writing, singing, exercising, and encouraging others. She holds an associate degree in early childhood care and education, a bachelor's degree in K-12 Special Education and Elementary Education, a master's degree in Teacher Leadership, and a doctorate in Curriculum and Instruction. One of her greatest passions is service and giving back to the community, which she does through several organizations in her local community. Her goal is to work with and inspire young mothers. If she could leave a quote to aid others, it would be, "Be sure that your faith is bigger than your fear. Always hold to your why."

missrofcc@gmail.com

Acknowledgments

First, I must thank my children.
My children gave me the space to grow and learn. They taught me faith, trust, and forgiveness. For this I am grateful.

Second, I must thank my mom.
    Look at you girl. Pat yourself on the back! You did it! You raised an author. I love you.

Lastly, but more importantly I thank God.
Without my relationship and belief in God, I would not have a relationship with my father.

Printed in Dunstable, United Kingdom